Homo erectus   Neanderthal   Cro-Magnon   Modern human

PREHISTORIC PEOPLE

By Bruce Coville

Illustrated by Michael McDermott

DOUBLEDAY
NEW YORK LONDON TORONTO SYDNEY AUCKLAND

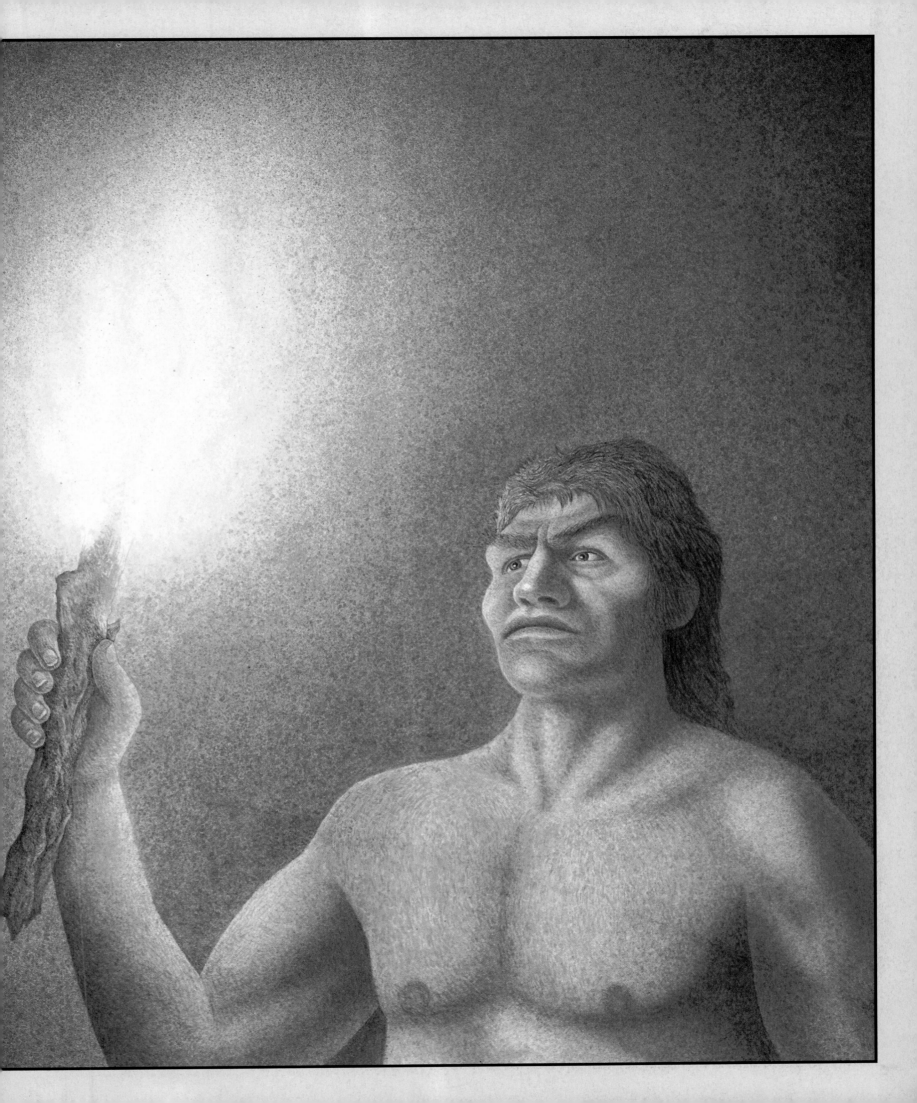

To Justin Coville
        —B.C.

Published by Doubleday,
a division of
Bantam Doubleday Dell Publishing
Group, Inc.
666 Fifth Avenue, New York, New York
10103

Special thanks to Dr. David R. Pilbeam
of the Peabody Museum, Harvard
University, for his careful review of the
manuscript and illustrations.

Library of Congress Cataloging-in-
Publication Data
Coville, Bruce.
   Prehistoric people.
   Includes index.
   Summary: Traces the development of
humans from Australopithecus to Cro-
Magnon, focusing on methods of
hunting and farming, artistic endeavors,
religious rituals, and technological
developments.
   1. Man, Prehistoric—Juvenile
literature. [1. Man, Prehistoric]
I. McDermott, Michael, ill. II. Title.
GN744.C67 1990 573.3 89-1549
ISBN 0-385-24922-5
ISBN 0-385-24923-3 (lib. bdg.)
RL:3.7

An Ancient Ancestor

A shaggy creature crouches in the heat of the African sun. In each hand it clutches a stone. Working quickly, it begins to strike one stone against the other.

When it is satisfied, the creature drops one stone. It stands. It has beetling brows and a great, outthrust jaw. But in its hand is an ax—a tool it has made to chop and cut, to dig up roots, to skin animals.

This creature, then, is not simply an animal. It is a human being. In fact, it is part of a long line of human beings that stretches from the ancient past directly to you and your family.

Who were these early humans? What were they like? How did they live?

And what do they have to do with us?

To learn the answers to these questions, we have to study clues our ancient ancestors left behind. Often these clues are small—little more than a tooth or a bit of bone.

But put together in the right way, they tell a fascinating story: the story of humankind.

A Difficult Question

"**W**here and when did human beings begin?" This is a question about which scientists love to argue. To answer it, you first must answer another question: Just what *is* a human being?

Scientists once defined humans as "those animals that make and use tools." Then it was discovered that chimpanzees make simple tools.

Another distinction was that humans use language. Then we learned that chimps and gorillas can be taught simple forms of language.

While some people would like to give chimps and gorillas legal rights and protections, most are not willing to call these distant cousins humans. So the definition was revised again. Now scientists say, "Humans *habitually* make and use tools. They master *complex* language."

Some students of early humans would choose another kind of definition. Humans are self-aware. They do not live only in the present, but think of the future. They understand that someday they will die. They have the capacity to wonder. They do not simply accept the world as it is. Instead, they look at it and ask, "Why?"

So perhaps the beginning of the human species came in the moment when one of our ancient ancestors looked up at the African sky and wondered why it had stars.

A chimp uses a simple branch as a tool to gather termites to eat

Early human (Cro-Magnon) using tools to eat

How Old Are We?

No matter how carefully we choose our definition, the precise dividing line between human and animal is hard to draw—especially in the distant past. As we will see, the steps that led from humanlike apes to apelike humans were taken very slowly, over millions of years. Today few scientists would choose a single moment and say, "This is the point where humans began."

To understand just how far back we must look to find our beginnings, imagine you have a pair of boots that will let you walk through time. If every minute you walk takes you a year into the past, it would take only a few minutes to pass the time when you were born. In less than an hour you would pass your parents' birthdays, perhaps even the time when your grandparents were born. In just over eight hours you would pass the time when Columbus first saw America.

If you could walk without stopping, without getting tired, still going back a year for every minute you travel, you would pass the beginning of recorded history in only five days.

But it would take you at least ten years to reach the time when the first *hominids* (humanlike creatures) appeared on earth.

Five days out of ten years: that's all the time for which we have written records. What happened during the rest of that time? And how do we know about it?

Clues of Stone

Even though our ancient ancestors did not leave written records of their lives, they did leave clues to the way they lived—clues made of stone.

Scientists who study these clues are called *anthropologists* (an-throw-POL-oh-jists). *Anthropo* means "human." *Logy* means "the science of." This makes anthropology "the science (or study) of humans."

Anthropologists learn about prehistoric people by studying traces of their lives that have survived to the present day.

Some of these clues are human bones that have been turned to stone by a slow process called fossilization. Other clues are the stone tools made by our ancestors. Because stone is not easily destroyed, such tools can survive a million years or more. They carry a message from the distant past—a message that tells about the person who made it.

Unfortunately, the further back in

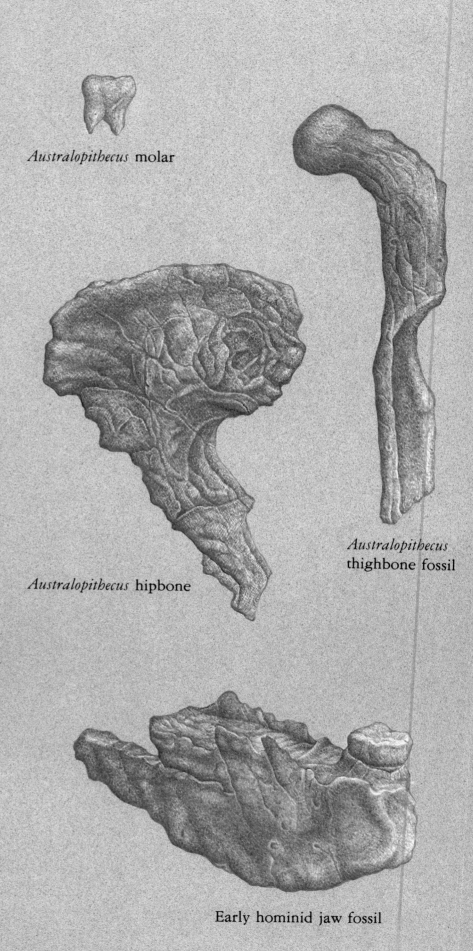

Australopithecus molar

Australopithecus hipbone

Australopithecus thighbone fossil

Early hominid jaw fossil

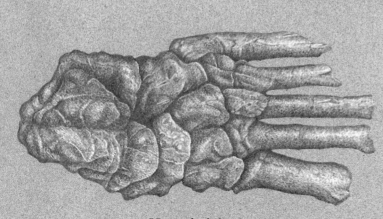

Homo habilis foot fossil

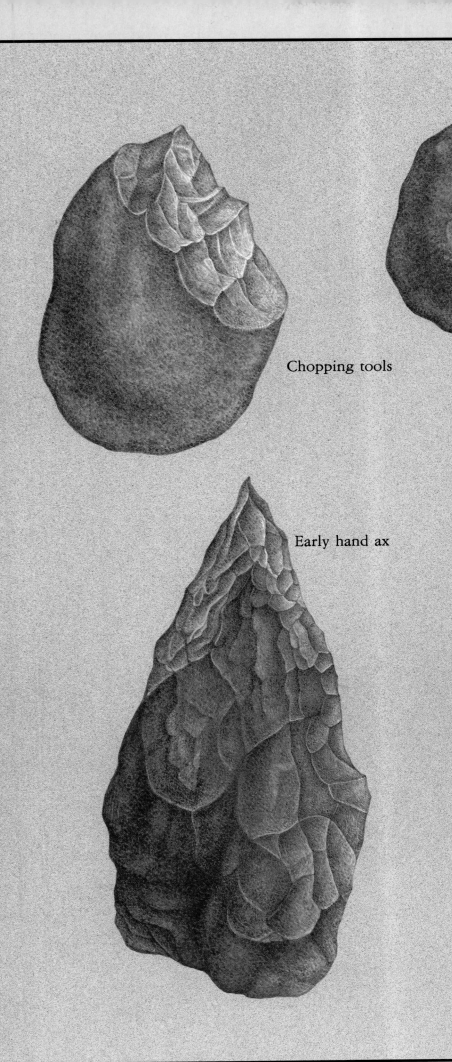

Chopping tools

Early hand ax

time we look, the fewer—and smaller—the clues become.

There are many reasons for this. First, of course, the more time that passes, the more likely it is that something will be destroyed.

Second, it takes very special conditions for a bone to become a stone fossil. Early hominids did not live in places where such conditions were apt to occur.

Third, when the earliest hominids began to make tools, they worked with little more than conveniently shaped rocks and sticks. Such sticks would not be likely to survive. An unshaped stone might not be recognized as a tool even if someone found it.

A fourth problem is that when hominids first began to walk the earth, they were very few in number—just a few small bands of humanlike creatures on the plains of Africa.

For these reasons, and many others, the fossil record of early humans is very sparse. Often scientists are forced to draw conclusions from little more than a chipped stone, a fragment of bone, and a few well-preserved teeth.

Ancient Tools, Modern Scientists

Anthropologists work in many ways. Some spend their time in far-off places, sifting through tons of dirt for the remains of prehistoric people.

Others work in modern laboratories. Here they use methods such as *Carbon-14 dating* to learn the age of finds made by others. Carbon 14 is a kind of radioactive carbon. It is found in all living things. This radioactive material decays at a steady rate after something dies. Therefore, measuring the amount that is left gives us an idea of how long ago the thing died. Unfortunately, Carbon-14 dating is useful only back to about 70,000 years ago.

Some researchers use electron microscopes to study *DNA.* Every living thing, including you, has DNA. It is like a blueprint, or plan, that tells your body how to grow. Half of *your* DNA came from your father, and half came from your mother.

By studying DNA, scientists can learn how things are related.

Other scientists take photographs of the *insides* of ancient skulls. These pictures help us understand the brains that were once inside those skulls. By comparing ancient and modern brains, scientists learn about how our ancestors' minds worked.

A scientist performs Carbon-14 dating to determine the age of fossilized bones

An anthropologist chips away the stone in which a bone of a prehistoric ancestor is embedded

Prehistoric Treasure Troves

Of course, such work would not be possible without the bits of stone and bone themselves. These things must be found "in the field," by scientists who sometimes devote their entire lives to digging for them.

One of the most famous fossil sites is Africa's Olduvai (OHL-duh-WAY) Gorge. Here Dr. Louis S. B. Leakey and his wife, Mary, found hominid remains about 2 million years old. These finds forced some scientists to rethink their theories about when human life began.

Another famous fossil site is Shanidar Cave, in the Zagros Mountains of Iraq. Here Dr. Ralph Solecki found the skeletons of eight prehistoric people. To do this, he dug through layers of material that had accumulated over a period of 100,000 years. Dr. Solecki's excavation was forty-five feet deep. His most remarkable discovery came at a level dated to 60,000 B.C. Here he found the remains of a caveman who appeared to have been carefully laid to rest on a bed of branches, then covered with flowers. This "flower burial" provided new clues to the way our ancestors behaved.

It takes both hard work and good luck for anthropologists like Solecki and the Leakeys to make such finds. Some very good scientists search for a lifetime without making a major discovery.

Age of Stone, Age of Ice

Discoveries by the Leakeys and others like them take us back to the earliest age of humankind. This era is known as the *Paleolithic* (pale-ee-oh-LITH-ick), or the "Old Stone Age." It is named for the primitive stone tools that people made at this time. The period lasted for over 2 million years.

Change was very slow in the Paleolithic. A new way of making tools might take a hundred thousand years or more to develop, or to spread from where it originated.

To understand the people of the Paleolithic, you must understand their world.

Imagine a land without buildings, roads, or power lines. The loudest sounds most people in this world will ever hear are the cries of animals and the occasional rumble of thunder.

There is no pollution. The water is clean; the air is pure. It is very beautiful.

But there are no stores or supermarkets. If you want food, you have to go out and find it. There are no cars or buses; in fact, there are no wheels. If you want to go someplace, you have to walk.

There is one more thing to know about this time: the world itself was constantly changing. The changes came so slowly that they did not affect any one generation of people. But over time, they caused changes to occur in our hominid ancestors.

These changes came about because the earth was in the grip of an Ice Age, which began about 2 1/2 million years ago. As the world's temperature dropped, water was periodically trapped in the ice caps. As these ice sheets or glaciers grew, layers of ice up to 10,000 feet thick came to cover large parts of the earth.

Though we refer to such times as Ice Ages, they were not a time of permanent winter everywhere. The whole world was cooler than it is now. But areas of the earth that are very hot today may have been quite pleasant in the Ice Ages.

Over these millions of years, the glaciers advanced and retreated many times. As they did, the climate changed. And as the climate changed, humans had to change to survive.

What kind of people lived in this world? A series of creatures that moved from something halfway between apes and humans to something fully human. Some of the hominids of the time proved to be evolutionary dead ends. These species moved past being apes, but never became fully human. Eventually they died out.

The fossil record of this time is like a jigsaw puzzle with many pieces missing. We know what these "ape-men" looked like, and something about how they lived. But exactly which ones were our direct ancestors is still a matter of great debate.

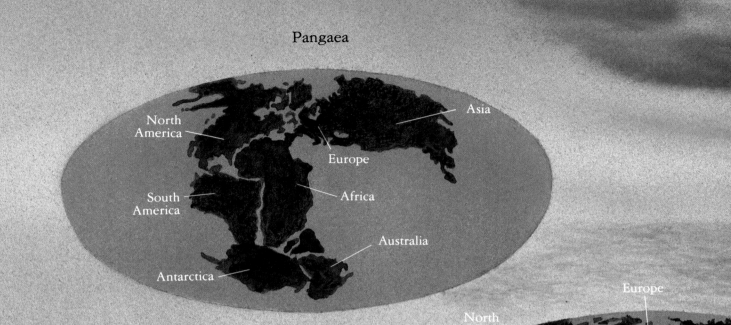

Pangaea

North America

Asia

Europe

South America

Africa

Australia

Antarctica

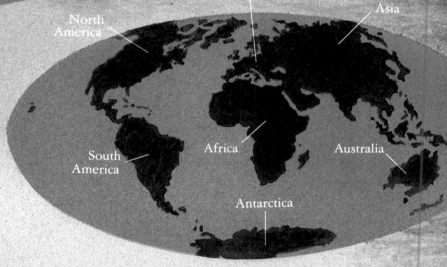

Europe

North America

Asia

South America

Africa

Australia

Antarctica

After continental drift

The Long Chain

Scientists will continue to argue about prehistoric people for years to come. However, most of them do agree on a few things. One is that the human species began in Africa.

But in truth, the deepest roots of human life go back to the beginning of life itself.

Life on earth dates back about 3 1/2 billion years. Some scientists believe that at this time the continents were grouped together in a single landmass they call Pangaea (pan-JEE-uh). The rest of the world—by far the largest part—was covered by one vast ocean.

Some scientists refer to that huge ocean as a "chemical soup." They believe that lightning striking the waters may have fused certain chemicals in ways that led to the first forms of life. These forms were very

Algae—the first forms of life

simple—tiny threads of bacteria and blue-green algae. But from them came all the kinds of life we see on earth today.

New forms of life develop through a process called evolution. In a way, life develops because of mistakes.

This may sound strange. But think about it. One of the basic functions of all living things is to reproduce—to create more living things like themselves. But if living things always reproduced themselves perfectly, there would never be any change. If the first forms of life had been able to reproduce themselves perfectly, they would be the *only* forms of life. They would stay exactly the same forever.

But mistakes do occur. Sometimes something grows in a different way. These changes, known as *mutations,* are not always good. Then the new kind of life does not survive.

But sometimes the change is an improvement.

Natural Selection

The prime tool of evolution is *natural selection.*

Natural selection means that some forms of life are better suited to survive than others.

Imagine a species of ape that lives on fruit. Fruit tends to grow on the ends of branches. So the longer an ape's arms are, the easier it is for it to gather fruit. Such an ape may be able to gather fruit other apes can't reach. When there is plenty of fruit, this may make no difference. But imagine a year when there is not enough fruit to go around —perhaps because the weather has been bad, perhaps because insects destroyed the fruit. Then the ape with long arms will have the best chance of getting enough food. Natural forces are "selecting" the apes with longer arms to survive. These apes are more likely to reproduce. And since the coding for

long arms is carried by DNA, the next generation of apes will probably have more infants with long arms.

With even occasional bad years, it wouldn't take long for the apes with long arms to become the rule rather than the exception. (Remember, when we are talking about evolution, "not long" can mean tens or even hundreds of thousands of years.)

Eventually, all the apes in this band will have long arms. If they are all equal in this way, some other trait may provide a survival advantage. For example, an ape that can see color may spot fruit other apes will miss. So this ape will have a better chance of surviving. And indeed, though color vision developed slowly, it is a trait primates have that most other animals do not. (*Primates* are the group of mammals that includes humans, apes, and monkeys.)

This is the way, over billions of years, that life evolved from simple cells floating in that first great sea to the wonderful diversity of plants and animals surrounding us today.

This is the way human beings came to be.

Our Family Tree

The beginnings of human life go all the way back to those one-celled bits of life floating in that first great ocean. That is where you will find the roots of every living creature in the world. This means that, in a way, every living thing is related. Dogs, cats, trees, and monkeys all had their beginnings in those distant bits of life. So did every other kind of life. So did we.

But obviously humans are vastly different from cats, or trees, or even monkeys. So where do *we* begin on this line of life?

Since humans are mammals, you might search for our beginnings at the beginning of the mammals.

The earliest, most primitive mammals evolved during the age of the dinosaurs, nearly 200 million years ago. These mammals were ground dwellers. But about 70 million years ago, a small, long-snouted animal—much like the tree shrew of today—left the ground to live in the trees.

Early tree-dwelling mammals evolved around 70 million years ago

Life above the ground provided strong evolutionary pressures. To survive in trees, you need to be able to hold on to the branches. It was here, many scientists believe, that some mammals first began to develop the separate, movable fingers that eventually led to the hands of apes and humans.

After a while, for reasons we are not sure of, some of these animals left the trees and returned to the ground.

This change provided new evolutionary pressures. Slowly, over millions of years, these pressures led to animals that could stand on their hind legs.

Now you can see how two traits may work together. Creatures who had strong, flexible fingers, and who could also stand up, had hands that were free to do other things—like make tools.

The individual steps in this chain are very unclear. While two fossils a million years apart may show the changes a species has undergone, what happened *during* those million years often remains a mystery.

Let's take a look at what we do know about the closer ancestors of man.

The Ancestral Apes

Sivapithecus

Twenty million years ago, early in the Miocene (MY-uh-seen) Era, Africa held a large variety of apelike creatures.

Scientists have found partial fossils of many of these apes. The earliest is called *Proconsul* (proh-KON-suhl). Like other apes of the time, Proconsul lived in trees and walked on all fours.

Later in the Miocene, 12 or 13 million years ago, lived an ape we call *Ramapithecus* (rah-mah-PITH-ih-kus). (*Pithecus,* which you will see in other names to come, is from a Greek word. It means, simply, "apelike.")

Ramapithecus weighed about thirty pounds. It lived in open forests at the edge of the grasslands. At one time anthropologists thought *Ramapithecus* was our ancestor. But recent fossil discoveries changed that theory. We now believe that *Ramapithecus* is part of another group of apes, called *Sivapithecus* (siv-uh-PITH-ih-kus). These Asian apes were not our ancestors after all; they are more like distant cousins.

This kind of rethinking is common in anthropology. When a new discovery is made, people often have to change their old ideas.

So what ape was directly ancestral to man? We may never know for sure. After the apes of the Miocene there is a gap in the fossil records. The gap begins about 8 million years ago. It stretches for 4 million years. On one

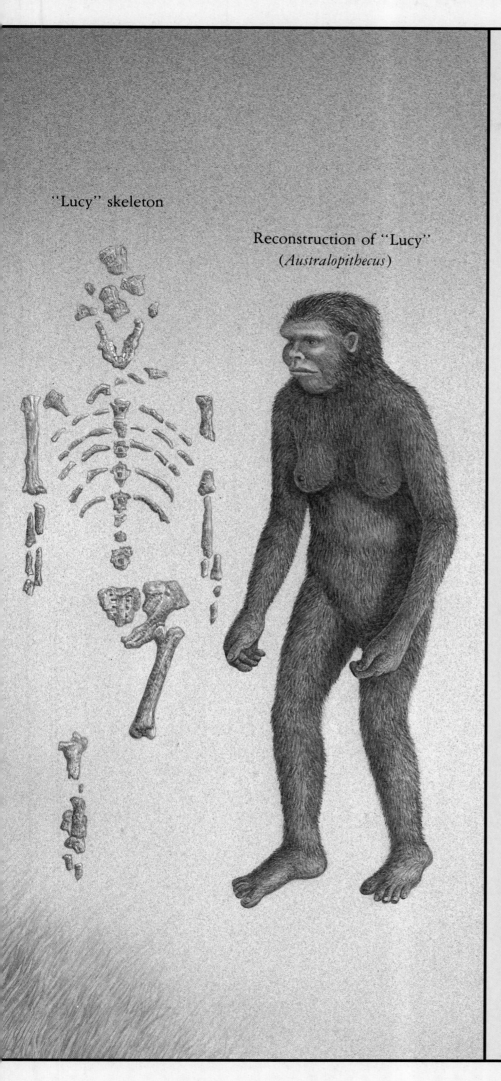

"Lucy" skeleton

Reconstruction of "Lucy"
(*Australopithecus*)

side of the gap is an ape—one of *Sivapithecus*'s African cousins—ready to develop into something more humanlike.

On the other side of that gap stands a creature that is neither ape nor human. Its scientific name is *Australopithecus* (aw-stray-low-PITH-ih-kus). Scientists have found the remains of many of these creatures. The most famous one of all is a little lady named Lucy.

Lucy is the name given to a skeleton discovered in Ethiopia in 1974.

Actually, the skeleton's official name is AL 288-1. But the discovery was so exciting that the people who made it stayed up late into the night, celebrating. Their tape player was blasting out the popular Beatles song "Lucy in the Sky with Diamonds." And so they decided to call the skeleton Lucy.

What made this discovery so exciting was that the skeleton was relatively complete. Scientists studying this time had been working from nothing but teeth and fragments of bone. Suddenly they had more information than they had ever seen for such an early ancestor.

Lucy stood about three and a half feet tall. Her head was probably about the size of a grapefruit. But she walked erect, not on all fours. She was not really human. But she was not merely an ape. She was a hominid.

The team that discovered Lucy was led by Dr. Donald Johanson. Dr. Johanson believes Lucy represents a common ancestor from which all later hominids evolved. As you would expect, others disagree with him.

But everyone does agree that Lucy is an early form of the species of hominid we call *Australopithecus*.

Australopithecus: The Ape-Man

Anthropologists first became aware of *Australopithecus* in 1924. That was when Professor Raymond Dart, of South Africa, was given a box of fossil-laden limestone. In the box he found the skull of a young primate. The skull was embedded in breccia, a mixture of limestone, sand, and gravel much like cement.

Working with first a chisel and then a sharpened knitting needle, Professor Dart began to chip away at the breccia.

It took seventy-three days of patient efforts to free the skull. For the first time in 2 million years, a modern man was looking at the creature we now call *Australopithecus.*

Professor Dart's discovery, which came to be known as the Taung Baby, set off one of the great battles of anthropology. It wasn't until fourteen years later, when other fossil hunters found similar skulls, that the picture began to clear.

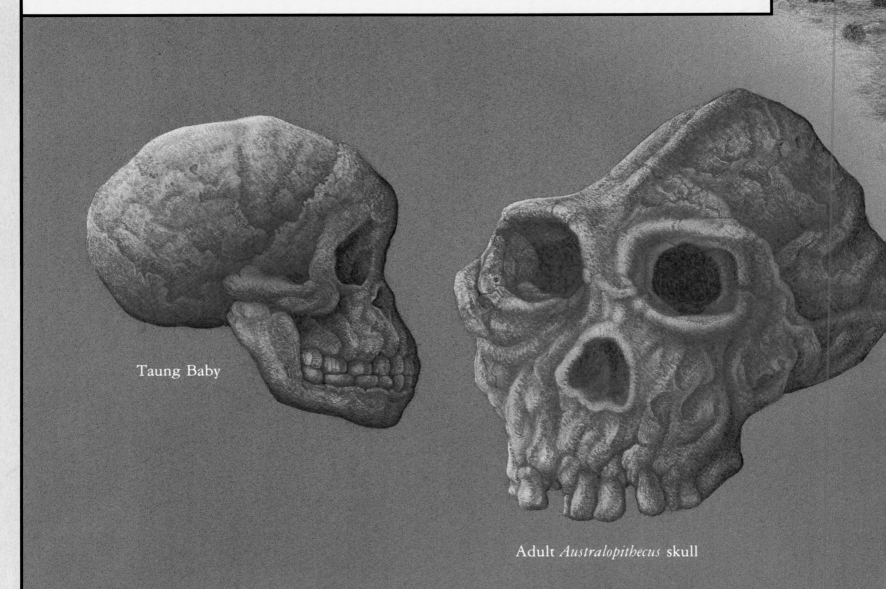

Taung Baby

Adult *Australopithecus* skull

As the first discoverer, Professor Dart had the right to name his new species. He called it *Australopithecus africanus,* or "Southern Ape of Africa." This did not turn out to be a very good name. We now know that *Australopithecus* lived in many places besides South Africa. Even more important, it was not an ape. It was a hominid.

The australopithecines (aw-stray-low-PITH-ih-seens) lived in the open. Most of their food came from plants, though they would eat meat if they found it.

Scientists have identified four kinds of *Australopithecus.* The largest, *Australopithecus robustus,* could reach five feet in height.

The average *Australopithecus* brain was about 500 cubic centimeters. Australopithecines were probably somewhat smarter than a chimpanzee. But it seems unlikely that they learned to make tools.

Anthropologists once thought *Australopithecus* was one of our earliest ancestors. Now it seems more likely that only one or two types of these creatures are related to us. The others were sidesteps along the road to modern humans. For reasons that are not clear, these other ancient cousins died out.

The Toolmakers

The great anthropologist Louis Leakey believed our earliest direct ancestor was a creature he called *Homo habilis* (HOH-moh HAB-ih-liss), or "handy man." Leakey believed *habilis* had lived further back in time than most other scientists felt was possible. He spent his life trying to find the fossils that would prove this belief.

As it turned out, Leakey was right; *Homo habilis* lived 2 million years ago. Even though these creatures were our direct ancestors, if you met one today you would not think it looked very human. The hominids we call *habilis* were only four to four and a half feet tall. They weighed no more than sixty pounds. They had low brows and outthrust jaws.

But they did something no other creature had ever done before: they made stones into tools.

Unlike many important fossils, the oldest *habilis* skull does not have a nickname. It is known simply by its museum code number: Skull 1470.

Skull 1470 was found by a group led by Louis Leakey's son, Richard Leakey. When they found it, the skull was in many small pieces. It took Richard's

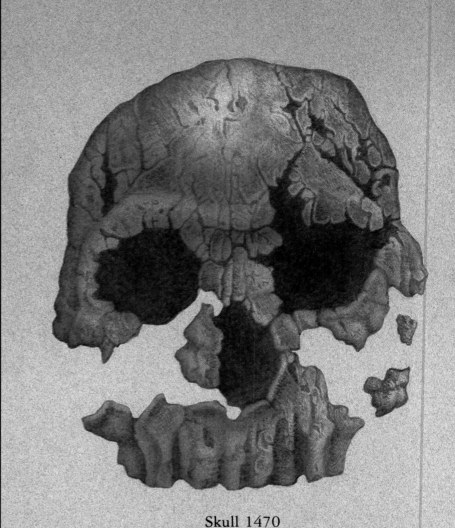

Skull 1470

Homo habilis tools

Hammerstone

Chopper

Cutting tool

Scraping tool

Flakes, blades

wife, Meave, six weeks to fit the pieces together.

The assembled skull was shown to Richard's father shortly before he died. It delighted the old man, for it proved that many of the theories he had been fighting for were true.

Homo habilis lived in small groups in the grasslands of Africa. They lived at the same time as the australopithecines.

Why did *Homo habilis* evolve into modern humans while the australopithecines died out?

No one knows for certain. Perhaps one factor was the ability to work together. Some scientists believe that *habilis* groups shared food. Rather than roaming, they established home bases— spots where they would camp for a time.

Not all scientists agree. But despite early theories about "savage ape-men," it now seems that cooperation may have been one thing that helped early humans survive.

The Upright Man

A short, hairy man puts a torch to some dried grass. Not far away from him, another man does the same thing. The grass fire spreads quickly, scaring a herd of enormous elephants. The great animals run in fear. The fire drives them toward a swamp, where their heavy bodies become stuck in the mud and the muck.

The men run in and kill the elephants. Tonight they will have a feast!

This is the way a scientist named Clark Howell interprets the evidence he found near Torralba (taw-RAHL-buh), a small village in Spain.

The scientific name for these men is *Homo erectus,* or "the man who walks erect." Although other mammals can do it for a brief time, only humans are designed to walk on their hind legs. Walking upright was an important step along the road that led to modern humans.

The average *Homo erectus* was shorter than a modern adult human—about five

feet tall. Their skulls were thicker. But their heads were considerably larger than those of earlier hominids. Their brains were twice as large as those of the australopithecines.

The first person to discover the remains of *Homo erectus* was a Dutchman named Eugène Dubois. Following his own theories of where such fossils might be found, Dubois went to Java, in the East Indies. With a combination of luck and skill that still astounds modern anthropologists, he found what he was looking for.

Dubois made his first finds in 1892. Though his discoveries were made in Java we now believe that *Homo erectus* first evolved in Africa.

One trait these early humans shared with modern people was a tendency to travel. *Homo erectus* left Africa and spread across much of the world. How long this took we do not know. But we have found remains of the species in China, Germany, Africa, and many other places.

The Neanderthals

I n 1856 an explosion shattered the quiet of a beautiful little German valley called Neanderthal (nee-AN-der-thawl).

The explosion itself was no surprise; workmen were using dynamite to blast away some stone. What was a surprise was the strange skeleton the explosion uncovered. This skeleton was certainly not that of an animal. But it was unlike that of any human that people of that time had known existed.

This was the modern world's introduction to *Homo neanderthalensis*. Members of this human species have since been found in many places throughout the world. But they were named for the little valley where they were first discovered.

It took a long time to understand the Neanderthals. Indeed, there is much about them that we still do not know. Their modern history illustrates a problem we have with interpreting the past: people often see what they want to see. The Neanderthals were very powerful people, with strong muscles and thick bones. It was easy for people who examined those bones to say the Neanderthals were stooped, hulking brutes. We know now that this is false —that those scientists were interpreting the evidence to fit their own viewpoint.

But the mistaken image of the stooped, brutish caveman lingered for a long time. In fact, it still shows up in some cartoons. When you see a cartoon like that, you can smile at the fact that the artist is working from ideas a hundred years out of date!

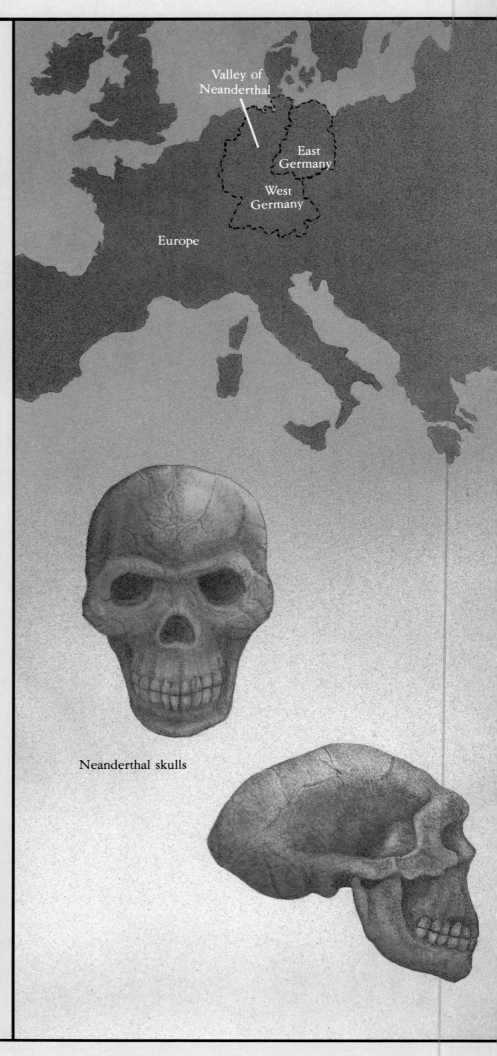

Valley of Neanderthal

East Germany

West Germany

Europe

Neanderthal skulls

Neanderthal man

The Neanderthal line began to evolve around 200,000 years ago. They were short, powerful people. Their skulls were low in front, with a heavy ridge of bone that made their brows jut out above their eyes. Though their noses were large and broad, they had barely any chin at all.

Despite what many people think, the Neanderthals were not stupid. In fact, some Neanderthal skulls have a brain capacity *larger* than that of modern humans. However, this does not mean they were smarter than we are. Intelligence depends not only on the size of the brain, but also on how the brain is organized.

The inside of Neanderthal skulls tells us that their brain was different from ours. This may mean they had different abilities. For example, their vision may have been better than ours. But some scientists suspect they could not think ahead as we do. This is because the section of the brain we use for that job was not well developed in Neanderthals.

Perhaps the parts of the brain that deal with language were less well developed in the Neanderthals. Some scientists believe that their throats could not produce a wide variety of sounds. So we suspect that their spoken language was not as effective as ours.

Yet in some ways the Neanderthals were surprisingly like us. For example, we know that the Neanderthals buried their dead. When someone is buried with food and tools, as was the Neanderthal that scientists call "the Old Man of La Chapelle" (after the place where his bones were discovered), it indicates a people who believed in an afterlife. So they may have had a kind of religion.

We also have evidence that the Neanderthals cared for sick and elderly members of their clans. For example, one skeleton that Ralph Solecki found in Shanidar Cave belonged to a forty-year-old man with a withered arm. His arm had been crippled from the time he was young. It seems unlikely such a man could have survived without the help of his clan.

Did they help him out of kindness, or because he had some special knowledge the clan needed? We cannot be certain. Whatever the reason, this evidence of group cooperation was a shock to those who believed the Neanderthals were nothing but cave-dwelling brutes.

These people had many skills. They knew how to make fire. They made tools from stone and bone. They used animal skins to cover their bodies and protect themselves from the cold.

Perhaps they even knew something about medicine. Some of the pollen found in the Shanidar "flower burial" comes from such plants as yarrow, hollyhock, and cornflower. Because people in that part of the world use these plants for medicine today, some scientists have wondered if the

Neanderthals also knew how to use those plants for healing.

The Neanderthals may have had many skills. But by about 30,000 years ago, their line had disappeared.

For a long time, we thought the Neanderthals were part of the long evolutionary road to modern humans. But most scientists now believe they were a detour—a sidestep that didn't work out. Like some of the australopithecines, the Neanderthals branched off, thrived for a time, and then disappeared.

What caused the end of the Neanderthals? Were they killed off by the surviving branch of the family tree? Did they die off because they were unable to compete for food? Or did they mingle with the newcomers, slowly disappearing as natural selection continued to favor the more successful group?

The end of the Neanderthal line is a mystery that anthropologists have not completely solved. However, they do have a clear picture of what came next.

Enter the Cro-Magnons

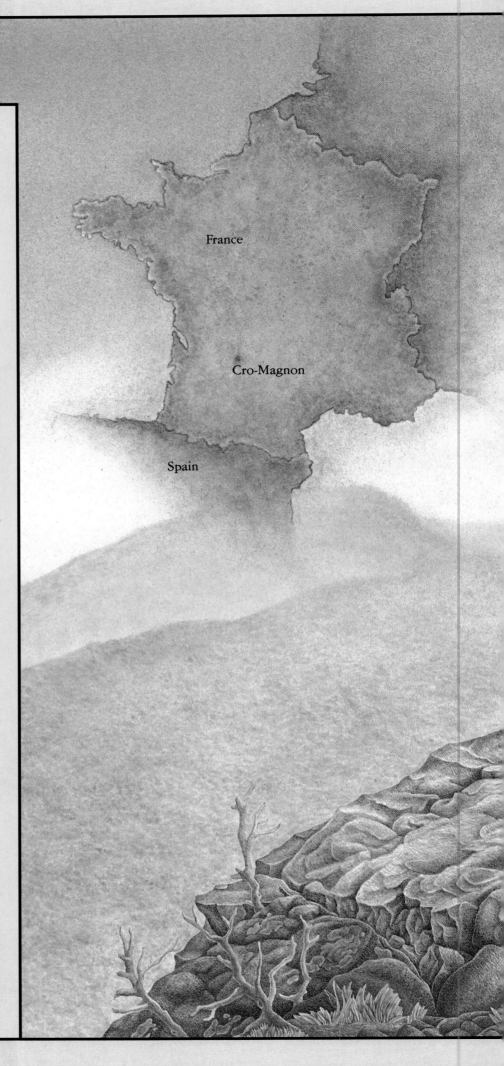

France

Cro-Magnon

Spain

Over 100,000 years ago, a new line of humans began to develop. Scientists refer to this branch of the family as *Homo sapiens,* which means "wise man."

Our first introduction to our nearest ancestors came in 1868, when French railroad workers discovered some skeletons near a rock shelter known as Cro-Magnon (krow-MAN-yon). As with the Neanderthals, we often refer to these people by the name of the place where they were first discovered.

The Cro-Magnons and the Neanderthals shared the world for tens of thousands of years. But about 30,000 years ago that changed. After the Neanderthals died out, *Homo sapiens* was the only kind of human left on earth.

And that is the way it has remained to this day. Every human alive today, including you, belongs to this species. Yet for all our vast numbers, in a way *Homo sapiens* is a lonely species. We are the only hominids left.

The Cro-Magnon people were a brainy group. In fact, their average brain size was *larger* than that of a typical human today. They were taller and more slender than the Neanderthals. From their skulls, we can tell that their faces looked much like ours. In fact, if you were to meet some

Cro-Magnons dressed in modern business clothing, you probably would not see anything at all strange about them.

These people were hunters. They were artists. They were dreamers and seekers and doers.

In short, they were much like us. And in their time, they invented much of what we consider the best of being human: music, art, and language.

Scientists have a saying: behavior leaves no fossils. A bone can be turned to stone and survive for millions of years. But a word or a movement cannot be saved like this.

Even so, we can make guesses about behavior from things that are left behind. For example, we know the Cro-Magnons made music from such items as a flute that was found in one of their caves. Carved from bone, this instrument has been dated to 32,000 years ago.

But such a discovery creates as many questions as it answers. We know Cro-Magnon people made music. But what kind of music? To look at such a flute is to wonder: What ancient songs our ears can never hear were played upon it? And what rhythms to which our feet can never dance accompanied it?

What was in the mind of Cro-Magnon men and women when they roamed the slopes of Ice Age Europe? What did they think, feel, believe?

And what led them to create the great artwork of such caves as Spain's Altamira (al-tuh-MEER-uh), and France's Lascaux (lahs-KOH)?

Deep in the Earth—Art!

On a September afternoon in 1940, four French teenagers made one of the greatest discoveries in the history of anthropology. The boys were planning to explore a cave they thought might hold the secret entrance to an old manor called Lascaux.

When the boys entered the cave, they found it was filled with wonderful paintings of horses, bison, and deer. Many of the images are enormous; the largest bison is about eighteen feet long. This is about three times the height of a tall man. The artists worked in four colors: red, black, brown, and yellow. The lines of the art are fluid and graceful.

These 17,000-year-old paintings are one of the greatest examples of art—prehistoric or modern—known to the world. When the famous artist Pablo Picasso visited Lascaux, he said, "We have invented nothing."

The Lascaux paintings are only one of many galleries of great cave art that have been found in Spain and France.

To paint in a cave you must have light. To provide this, our ancestors sometimes placed animal fat on a piece of sandstone. By adding a wick made of dried plant matter, they had something

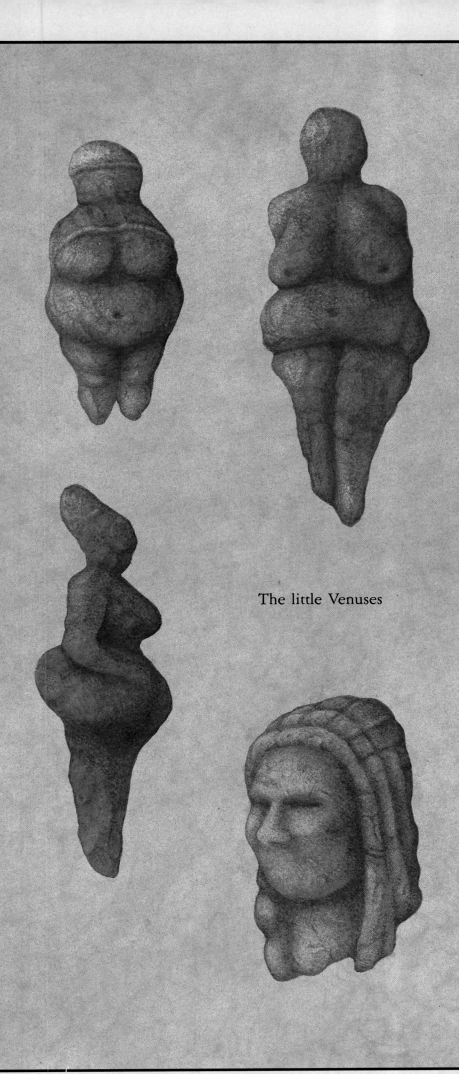

The little Venuses

that would function much like a modern candle. Charcoal found in the caves tells us they also used torches made of pine branches. They also made scaffolds—high platforms where these ancient artists could stand to paint upon the ceiling.

What was the purpose of this great art gallery? No one knows for certain. It may have been to initiate young men into the mysteries of the tribe. It may have had to do with hunting magic. The cave may have been a place to worship—a monument to the Ice Age gods not unlike our own great cathedrals.

Another kind of art associated with the Cro-Magnons is little statues of women. These statues are called Venuses, after the Roman name for the goddess of love. They have been found all across Europe and Asia.

The statues are often oddly exaggerated. The women shown may be very fat. They have no facial features—and no feet. Some scientists believe the statues were stuck into the ground.

What was the purpose of these little statues? Were they used in worship in some way? Did they represent some ancient goddess? Were they good luck charms, meant to bless the home, or the hunt?

We have no way of knowing for certain.

Whatever their purpose, they are one of the most widespread of all the remnants of our ancestors.

The Hunters

The earliest hominids were primarily vegetarians. It was easier to pick plants than to catch animals, although they may have been willing to eat dead animals that they found. But as humans developed, they learned the skills of the hunt.

As practiced by humans, hunting required tools, thought, preparation—and cooperation. In fact, it seems likely that cooperating and sharing are as basic to being human as flexible fingers and the ability to stand erect. The ability to cooperate was one of the things that helped bands of small, somewhat awkward hominids such as *Homo habilis* to survive.

The animals hunted by our ancestors included bison, mastodon, woolly mammoth, woolly rhinoceros, ibex, deer, and salmon. Also around—and hunted—were horses and different forms of cattle. What these people did not hunt were dinosaurs. The last dinosaur died tens of millions of years before the earliest hominid began to evolve.

In addition to hunting, humans could also be hunted. Other animals that shared the world with our prehistoric ancestors included such mighty hunters as the saber-toothed tiger and the dire wolf.

Hunters made wooden spears to kill their prey. Later they learned to use fire to harden the point. Even later they learned to make stone points to make their spears more effective.

Another method of hunting was to stampede a herd of animals over a cliff. In this way, a tribe could kill many animals at once. Such a hunt would provide far more meat than a tribe could use at any one time. Probably they had a great feast—and then spent a great deal of time drying meat to save for later. With mass kills, it is likely that much of the meat also went to waste.

We think of the Ice Age tribes as mighty hunters. But it is important to remember that they also ate many small animals—rabbits, birds, fish, and even grubs and lizards. They also ate fruits, roots, nuts, and seeds, which they would gather as they traveled.

The Farmers

Beringia

Areas of the world covered by ice

Areas of the world covered by land

Tribes of humans slowly made their way across the world, gathering food and hunting as they went. During some periods, much of the world's water was frozen into the glaciers. This made the seas very low, and areas that are now underwater were then dry land. During these times, North America and Asia were connected by a continent-sized strip of land scientists call Beringia. This is how prehistoric humans first came to the Americas.

Most tribes continued to make their living as hunters and gatherers. But about ten thousand years ago, people in the Middle East made a remarkable discovery. They learned to grow their own food.

It is hard to pinpoint exactly when this happened. Probably it happened gradually, like most changes of this time. Remember, something that seems obvious to us may have been a great mystery to our ancestors. For example, we all know what seeds are for. But when—and how—did humans first learn this? Did they notice that when they

spilled certain seeds, plants would later grow in that spot? Or did someone notice that when seeds they had collected got wet, some of them began to sprout?

We do not know for sure. But we do know that the people who figured these things out changed the world. Why?

Well, farming requires people to stay in one place. Farmers become tied to their land in a way that roving bands of hunters are not.

With farming, a new kind of community is created. As these communities grow, they may provide a surplus of food. If there is more than enough food to go around, some people can do other things besides grow food. They can become potters, weavers, or priests.

Homes, once temporary structures for convenience, now take on more importance. Because they stay in them longer, people want to make them larger and more comfortable.

And "man the farmer" becomes "man the builder."

The End of Prehistory

The more people know, the faster changes occur. In the Paleolithic, it sometimes took 100,000 years, or more, for a new way of making tools to be completely developed. But as time went on, as our prehistoric ancestors learned to use fire, the wheel, and the bow and arrow, the pace of change grew faster. (This is still happening today. Our technology may change more in one year than that of our prehistoric ancestors did in a thousand centuries.)

As people learned more, they felt a need to keep track of it. This job sometimes fell to a tribe's priests. Among other things, a priest was supposed to keep track of the seasons, of the movements of the sun and the stars.

In the human mind, need leads to invention. The priests' need to keep track of things may well have led to their inventing a system of marking things down, so they didn't have to keep everything in their heads.

Our first written records come from ancient Sumer (SOO-mer), which is part of the country now called Iraq. The Sumerians (soo-MEER-ee-uns) made marks in tablets made of wet clay. These tablets were then baked, in order to harden them. This made them very permanent—much more permanent, in fact, than the paper on which most books are printed.

These clay tablets are 5,000 years old. For the first time we have the words and thoughts of ancient people recorded for us to share. They represent the beginning of history—and the end of the prehistoric era.

Or is it really over?

The Living Stone Age

In 1971 a man named Manuel Elizalde, Jr., led an expedition to the Philippine island of Mindanao. The expedition made an astonishing discovery—a tribe of people called the Tasaday who seemed to have had no contact with the modern world.

The Tasaday lived in caves. They made stone tools from pebbles found in the streams near their cave. They were, in effect, a Stone Age tribe, living in the fashion of people tens of thousands of years ago.

Scientists also know of some tribes in Africa who live in the old way, even though they have had contact with the modern world. These tribes include the pygmies, a race of people known for the fact that rarely does an adult grow taller than five feet. They also include the !Kung Bushmen. (The exclamation point indicates that the !Kung speak a special "click language.")

By studying people who live this way today, anthropologists can make guesses about how prehistoric people may have lived.

One of the most interesting things about these tribes is that while they do not have the material wealth most of us take for granted, they often seem to be happy and well fed. They actually have more leisure time than people living in a "civilized" fashion.

The life of these modern Stone Age tribes is utterly different from our own. Yet they are fully human, and there is much we can learn from them.

The Human Question

From the first tiny bits of life floating in the early sea to the wonderful variety of life surrounding us today there stretches a fascinating, intricate web. You are part of that tapestry of life, as is every living thing that can be found on the earth today.

But though we are part of the web, we are also something special, something like no other creature on earth.

Each species has its own special survival tools: fangs or claws, great speed, the ability to hide, the ability to withstand drought. Our tools are our brain and our hands. And these tools give us a power no other creature has ever had: the power to shape and change the world around us in whatever way we choose.

But they leave us with a great question: How *will* we shape the world?

Will we make it better—or will we destroy it?

We are the only creature that has ever had that choice.

And that, too, is part of what it means to be a human being.

Index

About the Author

Bruce Coville is the award-winning author of more than twenty books for children and young adults. He has also contributed to numerous magazines and newspapers including *Sesame Street Parent's Newsletter* and *Cricket.*

Mr. Coville is a graduate of the State University of New York at Oswego and a former elementary school teacher. He is now a full-time author, and writes from his home in Syracuse, New York.

About the Artist

Michael McDermott grew up with a love for drawing and painting. He studied at the Maryland Institute College of Art and graduated with a desire to enter the field of children's book illustration in 1986. Since that time he has worked as a freelance illustrator in both advertising and publishing. This is the artist's third book for children.

He lives with his wife in Stewartstown, Pennsylvania, in a 150-year-old house which they are in the process of restoring.

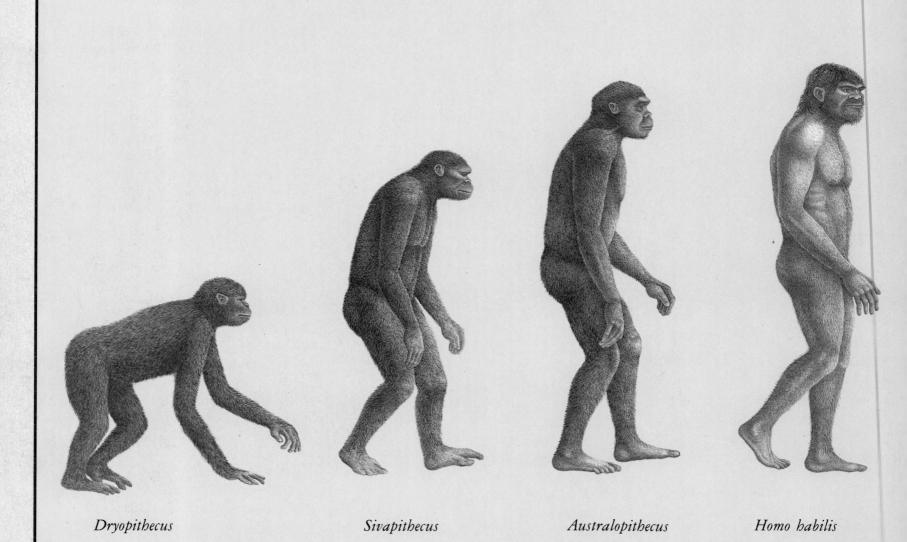

Dryopithecus   *Sivapithecus*   *Australopithecus*   *Homo habilis*